*Books by Deborah Digges*

LATE IN THE MILLENNIUM    1989

VESPER SPARROWS    1986

*Late in the Millennium*

/

# Late in the Millennium

DEBORAH DIGGES

ALFRED A KNOPF

NEW YORK   1989

THIS IS A BORZOI BOOK
PUBLISHED BY ALFRED A. KNOPF, INC.

Grateful acknowledgment is made to the following magazines in which the poems in this book were originally published:

AGNI: "Tartarchos," "Hall of Souls"
ANTAEUS: "Resurrection Garden"
FIELD: "The Sea with Doors"
MISSOURI REVIEW: "Media Years"
THE NEW YORKER: "To the Angels," "First Fire of the Season," "Secrets," "Circadian Rhythms," "Sycamores," "For the Second Millennium," "The Rockettes," "The Flower Thief"
Poets for Life, Crown Publishers: Faith-Falling"
PEQUOD: "A Greeting," "Oaxacan Stories"

My deepest thanks to the National Endowment for the Arts and the John Simon Guggenheim Foundation whose generosity gave me the time and the peace to write. Special thanks to Harry Ford. The epigraph was taken from Heidegger's lectures entitled On Building, Dwelling, and Thinking. Some of the information used in "The Hokey-Pokey" came from Gregg Easterbrook's "Are We Alone?," The Atlantic Monthly, August 1988.

Library of Congress Cataloging-in-Publication Data

Digges, Deborah.
    Late in the millennium : poems / Deborah Digges. — 1st ed.
      p.    cm.
    ISBN 0-394-58067-2
    ISBN 0-679-72595-4 (pbk.)
    I. Title.
PS3554.I3922L3   1989
811'.54—dc20
                                89-45309
                                    CIP

Manufactured in the United States of America
First Edition

*For Eva*

*To build is to dwell.*

# Contents

*For the Second Millennium*   3

*The Flower Thief*   5

*Circadian Rhythms*   7

*Resurrection Garden*   9

*First Fire of the Season*   11

*Oaxacan Stories*   12

*The Rockettes*   15

*Sycamores*   16

*The Bitter Withy*   18

*A Greeting*   19

*The Hokey-Pokey*   25

*To the Angels*   27

*Tartarchos*   29

*Secrets*   31

*Hall of Souls*   33

*To Science*   35

*Media Years*   36

*Idaho Plates*   39

*The Sea with Doors*   40

*House*   42

*Faith-Falling*   44

*Kingdom, Phylum, Class, Order, Family, Genus, Species*   46

*Late in the Millennium*

# For the Second Millennium

## 1

If one life were enough or eternity
    had seasons
and were somehow translatable, glacial,
an enormous braille, or simply scored, a scar, its story,
    then you could pan the body-waters
    for those gold tokens, those tiny arms and legs,

heads, hearts, hands, feet, each affliction
    in strict relief
on the sanctuary wall, each soul, if we have one,
in detail, meaning: *after the beating she would not heal* . . .
    or, *like the earth*
    *I have made stones inside me*

to which I've moored myself,
    *little grief harbors— set me, set me asail* . . .
When Guadaloupe's cathedral door
swung open nearly twenty years ago, I saw them startle,
    shine above the many candles
    lit for the sick, the lost,

the compassed cloud of witnesses,
    as though pain could be light's companion
out on some sea
among the huge schools of mackerel
    that surface in the swells, flash and dive
    in unison into the nets

to be hauled up, hauled in along the shore.

## 2

Tonight across the channel
the robot lighthouse beam takes in this island.
Though it's late in the twentieth century,
if you watch closely,
you can make out a man, above the tide-line,

sweeping the sand with a contraption
that listens for buried treasure,
coins like the ones in the new airports'
or shopping malls' terrariumed, sky-lit tile fountains
which buy a midnight janitor
his cigarettes and coffee.

As for the wishes the coins are proof of,
they seem sometimes to hover
when the crowds pass, fanning the water, blurring
their own reflections, as though later,
airborne above the city, outbound,
or driving home, the donors,

self-blessed, simply for wishing,
greeted more easily the future
carried in the blood, some gene-remembering,
prophetic news, that by the light of synaptic fire calls back
a thousand generations.

# The Flower Thief

Who watches behind curtains her landlord counting his hundred
or so jonquils, or fingering like a scout the dogwood's
five or six snipped branches knows the fugitive's
lust for the wayward tea rose bobbing above the hedges.
She's cased all winter the sidewalk gardens. She's gone
at dusk among forsythia and lilacs, the curb-side gutters

petal-clogged, the tulip trees' sprung husks pouched as gutted
fish. There the streets are littered with the blossoms of a hundred
redbuds blown and drifting like confetti after the parade's gone
by. As if she were a part of that great wedding and would
greet them at the threshold, she clips the ripest from the hedges,
and for herself a few studded golden sheathes, just a fugitive's

provisions, enough to set in jars on the leeward sills like fugitive
fires along a bluff above the sea, the camps stone-cold, gutted
by dawn, as clueless as the next, each bud anonymous, the donor hedge
in one moon-phase replete. Who'll know the difference in a hundred
years or care she spends them all in rented rooms? The green wood
tears away. Her hands are pollen-stained and dewy, and gone

at last are any traces of remorse, any self-promised penance, gone
as the roses she once threw to an old matador whose fugitive
soul she thought she'd always love and, grown up, someday, would
come back to. Another year she'd stood before the shit-gutted
cage of an orangutan, his floor a wash of how many hundred
fuchsia blossoms he'd stripped from the hydrangea hedges

within reach. Now he scooped up petals like a miser—his hedges
half-blighted—then washed his face in flowers, his eyes gone
tired with wonder or forgetting deep in the scent, in one of hundreds
of northern coastal towns where winter's long and summer's fugitive.
So she runs, cradling her cache, clearing the bright gutters,
and backs along a wall out of the streetlight and jumps the wooden

fences laddering the terraces sentried by oaks, beechwood,
and sycamores. Their tufty seeds, miles away, swarm the asphalt hedges.
Their rent, exhausted blossoms funnel down the harbor gutters,
or drift, too light to sink, across the bay, like small armadas going
home from some new world. The flags go up. Out on the fugitive
horizon, the crew will not look back at us, the hundreds

waving from the shore, hundreds turning toward these gutted store-
     fronts
by the fugitive light, our faces pale as woodbine above the hedge
of traffic. The flower in her hair grows seedy, star white. Then she's
     gone.

# Circadian Rhythms

In Port Angeles' one library
one early March morning, we put our heads down,
weary, on a desk and slept an hour before

driving on along the coastline,
which looked never-peopled, and at the same time
domestic, with its pools of palm-sized

round blue stones, its bleached
up-ended trees, their huge root-masses hosting webs
of mussel-studded seaweed

that, lifting a little in the wind, sparked
signals leeward.
I'd never been as happy,

maybe because, as Darwin says, my own salt blood
sang greeting, for the first time,
to its primordial birthplace,

that shore washed by the tides.
And we'd just come to each other from a great distance,
across a thousand miles of steaming,

half-frozen ancestral soil
whose ragged furrows along the hills' arcs
looked like the scoring in ancient pots

that retain, they say, in each crevice,
the sound of the wheel grinding
and the potter keeping time and the village alive around him—

we'd come to each other still lost,
irreparably damaged.
But in the months of our first loving,

we believed we'd been made whole,
at least a small wing's
width of light in some bird's dreaming itself

back across the continent,
at least a part of the infinitesimal turning
that sends a hundred species skyward,

sends them home,
though they fly, sometimes, into air so cold
it kills them,

into fields so stripped they'll starve among the weeds.
But isn't it instinct's greatest vision
to extend what's possible,

to risk not coming back,
the way light, bending in water, disappearing,
wakes all the colors of earth?

I'll miss you,
and miss your hands on me,
while all the dead nests this autumn unravel

in the trees.
Here the sky is a rare blue, a deep, endearing chaos.
It could be spring beyond our understanding.

# Resurrection Garden

Five weather-beaten hives line the north ridge
like battened cottages along a dune.
The ground down the wide hillside's not yet grass
but a tightly knotted wool, its brown to light-
brown nap so subtle, save the occasional relief
of obvious loose green, the weaver went blind with detail.
The staggered thousand trees have only budded.
You can see through their dead nests to the pond.
In fact, its cloud-colored water, almost a circle,
is distracting, the way hearing
someone in a crowd suddenly sing or cry out
becomes all you can remember of a year.
To the south, right off the tracks,
a child once staved a lean-to
with whittled saplings against a limb.
Just now the orchard's like a sculpture garden.
The random tarred stumps say its maker
had ambition, a gift for closure.
Even the scattered wood looks to be arranged.
A few blighted, bony apples coming in July
should probably be bronzed and sent to a museum
and left to feed the common birds,
each species so precisely like its ancestors,
it seems they've forfeited the notion of a soul.
Autumns, drunk on rot, they'll dive into the pond's
first freeze, their wings splayed like lyrebirds
by December between layers, along with a diminished
rabbit or raccoon that, thirst-crazed some sunrise,
mistook for earth the mud-fuzzed ice, fell through.
What desperate surprise! What bobbing,
clinging to an edge that keeps coming away slush!
The spring we found my red boots
floating on the pond, it was as though I had come back
as someone else to the commemoration
of an ancient tragedy made festive,
among the blossoms, through re-enactments,

9

a tour-guide's sing-song lines: *and just as the burning*
*cattails closed a circle around the pond,*
*her father called to her* (with emphasis)
*get off the ice!*
Then the drift, the cold slide under,
the sun, without analogy, an otherworldly green . . .
As, just this morning, the Atlantic
and a continent away, I wandered, jet-lagged,
through a gallery past fallen archways
and tortoises of stone and stone sarcophagi
that carried the medieval fisherman and all his saints
beyond the Renaissance's enlightened harbors,
until I came to the twentieth century,
its early Pollocks, the wall-sized silk reactors
of the triptych "Sword of the Pig," "A Bigger Splash," Magritte's
eternal skies lit beyond "Venus of the Shaving Brushes,"
the last exhibit anything wooden:
pieces of yokes and charred mangers, wheel-spokes, oars,
axe handles, then ladles, spoons,
and honey dippers arranged in descending sizes
like a bridge, distanced, bolted to the floor.
And suddenly homesick, I knelt down there.
Could I cross over? Must I walk around?
as though the guard in the corner weren't part
of the sculpture, and his shadow, and the locked
door behind him, through the key-
hole the room utterly empty.

# First Fire of the Season

Blessed is the word igniting now
under the green spitting wood alive with insects.
Blessed the names, dissembled, falling,
blessed their miraculous erasures.
How quickly a nest would burn this evening, the shell-

embedded down, the underweavings.
How quickly become a fist of fire opening
mid-air, plummeting.
When I was a child a falling star meant *someone's dying*—
the terrible luck of knowing

seeding the dark, growing like prophesy,
as if some distant farmhouse light had gone out
for good in the imagination, some bird
jumped in its sleep, feeling
the dead pull of the migration.

# Oaxacan Stories

Tonight your father brings down from the mountains
    a secret hidden in a hassock
under piñatas and cheap pottery bowls,
    and when he's soaked it a week
        in the big sink in the basement,
    rolled its teeth like dice and brushed them clean
        of the ancient clay,
    he lets you help him wire the jaw

    together, work its mouth to greet you
        from another century, then toss that small skull
hand to hand to gauge, he says, how tall was this
    lost wanderer, a little wind
        from his juggling stirring the naked
bulb, his features suddenly articulate
    against a condor-shadow,
    which is why, in his orchards,

    you pretend you are orphans
        building lean-tos along some bough
below the tracks, where you watch for hobos to leap
    from the trains, their dead fires scarring
        the sandstone by the pond, a piece of mossy shirt
no less to you than the glass
        from their whisky bottles you hold to your eyes
    like spectacles toward the afterlife

    of color, brown sky, clouds, the sun
        in sepia gone timeless,
and if, before sleep, you put your faces in your hands,
    feel the bones that are anonymous
        as charred wood scattered on a shoreline,
    some stranded tribe long since moved
        inland, following the flocks like Siegfried, who,
    tasting the heart of a dragon,

knew the language of birds,
            so hacked a life out of the thickets,
out of the earth itself, a room whose window framed the faces
        of the enemy only the blood
                remembers, it is to practice this loving for nothing
        but the future: here are your brothers smiling
                in photographs
                above their first cadavers,

            and here your sisters, broken
                into women, entering another stranger's dream,
and here's the story of twelve of you
        grown up, alive at once, walking
                the summer orchard
        that, by some trick of nature, blossomed, in spite
                of a late freeze,
                and it's as though you've come

            to the end of your beliefs
                to see those trees aswarm with kingbirds, jays,
and waxwings, sparrows, robins, swallows, starlings, feeding
        in the top branches,
                or broadcast, where the fruit rots
on the ground, a thousand or more calling back
                in the racket of wings and leaves
                the long line of extinctions, premonitions,

            the great mythical birds—
                it's as though from now on whatever holds you, beauty
or failure, the litany
        of one another's names,
                whatever holds
        you means to let you go,
                the flesh already slackening on your big Dutch
                moralistic bones,

your parents turning back to the house
you were born in, not without waving, not
without stumbling over the onion grass
less than a mile from the place you stood on someone's
shoulders, for the first time finding your echo,
and called and called toward the river,
and that night and for sometime after slept poorly,
woke crying for the ones lost on the other side.

# The Rockettes

My mother danced with the Rockettes one spring
just to earn, she said, a little extra
money after her daytime job nursing

the sick in their homes, some of them dying
during the night. They called her Geneva.
She kissed them, danced with the Rockettes one spring.

Each time she locked arms she had a saying,
*Compassed about with so great a cloud . . . a*
repertoire of greetings, smiles, bows. Nursing

required it, and getting through an evening
knowing *any minute now*. Stamina!
So she danced hard with the Rockettes one spring.

And in Missouri, years inland, she'd sing
to the cancan over our wild hurrahs,
lift high her long, lovely legs, old nursing

cap flying, as though she were rehearsing
with her six daughters, who shouted *Vive la
vie!* as we danced like the Rockettes one spring—
breathless, she rocked the baby, flushed, nursing.

# Sycamores

As if their height had taught them this startling
      shyness, like a boy grown
      taller than his mother, the sycamores
have turned not quite a handful of colors.
      They make me think of the years I've lived
      on false hope, the wrong

      questions, sending my children out
      each morning like mortal
      wishes, smiling, waving.
Then desolate in their absence I lay down whole
      days and slept. Once when I drove to California,
      a shirt tied by its arms to a tree became

      all I couldn't love, or could not, myself,
      be loved by.
      Before you can let go there is this last
terrible embracing. One winter I loved a boy years younger
      than I am. In his arms,
      like leaning against the saplings

      of my childhood, I used to watch the ageing
      sun usher into our room
      bird shadows and the softened, twiggy shadows
of the tops of trees, and swarm his thin face
      as he went easily inside me, smiling,
      since he knew what I watched.

      Now when I remember him
      like so many strangers mouthing directions,
      over and over, until I've reached
my destination, or, stuck in traffic, hear
      some cheap love song so deeply, I'm silenced,
      I think our lives hold many futures,

each one as random, as intended,
          the way two friends of mine met accidentally
          in a foreign city, and shared a meal,
and came to love each other. Among the passionate contrasts
      of the enduring world, among
          the dogwoods and sumacs, scarlet maples,

birches, the sycamores are almost
          empty this morning, their white limbs highest
          against the blue November sky
as though they'd been called back already through
      the sarcophagi's stained wood
          and the house on fire and the shipwreck

drifting shoreward and the locked
          door, like the trees of the afterlife,
          here, along this hillside,
and their numerous, enormous, unflattenable leaves.

# The Bitter Withy

Love is all, love's never enough.
Then one's futures shut down like a playhouse roof.
Once I finally grew into my sister's
favorite shoes only to lose them in the orchard.
Say the dogs carried them off.

They used to bury sinners at the crossroads
far from the hilltop churchyard's hallowed ground.
What soul could find its way, then, caught
up in the thermals, or follow,
after the rains, the grey-green leaf-

stains scattered on the stone?
I followed them home this morning,
the first autumn in eighteen years without you.
Outside the willow's mother-
shadow, why is it happiness has left no scar?

# *A Greeting*

What's more ghostly
    than music? The air raid
sirens begin their deafening diphthong, finding C
    sharp,
        finding in me
the song played out each time I sat
        with the other children along a school's
    inside wall, all of us

    obedient to those
      useless rehearsals.
We were born in that line-up in 1950— most,
    on the sandbagged banks
      of the Missouri, who breathed
the air of the first fall-out. That flood's recorded,
      dated, signed by its
    witnesses above the windows

    of some bottomland houses,
      the river
made mortal
    as history under
      an infant's heel. That year three-
million four hundred thousand babies
      inherited America. The hospitals
    ran out of room,

    and the census takers,
      who wrote the rolls on anything—old
envelopes, receipts
    marked *paid in full,* train
      schedules—.
The joke's pedestrian.
      To find ourselves we might as well have looked
    into the sea,

as into the new hearth
of the tv screen
on Sunday nights
when *Twentieth Century* viewed railroad
cars crammed full
of bodies, viewed, *in the twinkling of an eye,*
the empty ocean
that was Nagasaki,

saw finally, in 1970,
the very future spun
out of the hopper like a wheel
of fortune.
A man sang out the birthdays—the prizes,
exile, wheel-
chairs, death warrants,
mindlessness.

But back home, the evenings
took the overgrown orchard,
the light lifting,
catching in the leaves. The convent bells
on the west
side of town called
the young nuns to vespers through their
paradise

gardens,
and rang for the local
casualties, at first less
than an octave's
scanning. After supper, we'd
go outside
to listen, sprawl
out on the new

sod covering the bomb
    shelter, its plot half-
starved, white-yellow at the borders, islanded
    among the chickweed rashes,
        dandelions.
    And sometimes we crawled under
            the evergreens' dwarfed forest past
        where the dogs

        had dug cool places in the dust.
            The window well, say,
four by four by eight,
    was a familiar grave for
        fledglings, rabbits. Letting ourselves
    down among
            their bones, we
        cupped our faces,

        like thieves,
            against the chlorophyll-
streaked glass until
    the newspaper
        bundles inside, cartons of winter
    coats and Christmas decorations took on the cold
            clarity
        of prophecy: you'd

        let yourself into a house
            one day
and find everyone gone, taken up
    in *the rapture*, or moved,
        without you,
    underground.
            After the war some vets came home
        only to disappear

into the rain forests. If
you can find them,
pick them out against the lichen's
silvery explosions, the ancient stock-
piles of
gangliated green, they'll tell you
the names of all
the trees, which

ones are good for burning, building, or
they'll part, like a
cloud, the ferns' floors,
show you tiny, medicinal weeds. Then
it's as though the jet
trails clearing
those mountains—called after the gods'
dwelling places—

were tethered
at the horizon, like the horseflies
Cambodian children on the six o'clock
news tied up below
the wings and let loose over the empty air-
fields, until the lines
sagged, or were torn suddenly from
their hands.

It's as though history
were an engine without
lights, without imagination, dragging its ghost
cargo, like
the shadows of planes. Who
in the next millennium will catalogue
those ships, make
sense of their

destinies, drawn
                from the things of this
world in the arbitrary stars—fire signs,
            water—poured
                out of the little dipper?
            It's true we never said a proper good-bye, never
                greeted
                one another.

            So welcome
                to the planet, babyboomers, welcome.
Time's lyrical, though
            the compass cannot be
                altered where we find ourselves, say,
            at a table,
                toasting the past, toasting
                the future, free

            for a moment, of the hard
                collective truths, oaths
broken, binding, free
            of the complicity inherent in surviving. Now
                the media turns its
            aging face,
                like a globe, toward our
                numbers as we

            run in special
                jogging suits past the homeless along
a river, or lift our children up, as once we longed
            to be lifted,
                to see the strobe lights
            flashing, vectoring
                in the planes that flare
                out a little above

the earth, touch down with startling
grace onto the runways. We were conceived
of something as simple as desire,
of fathers turning in the dark from women changed, born
of the dream that still wakes them
in their old age, as they look
back on us, waving from the dead
middle of our lives.

# The Hokey-Pokey

Look, the leaves are changing, and all
over the neighborhood, in apartment house front
   yards, on balconies, the booths go up,
      just two-by-fours and siding.
The entrances are flowered bedsheets someone's
   made love on, surely, or, lying
against a wall, hugged himself to sleep.
   Evenings below the roar of inbound jets,
      their landing lights visible
for miles, below a children's record,
   "The Hokey-Pokey," blasting from the retirement
home's basement windows, you can hear
   the men inside their *sukkot* in the language
      of the ancestors singing what saved them
in the wilderness. Yesterday my half-
   grown son and I carried a dollhouse
from the curb, and painted and repaired the roof,
   the broken stair, papered the walls
      with remnants from our old clothes
from all the houses we remember.
   It was a kind of worship, one of us sooner
or later a witness to the other's faith.
   Turning to dress, one year, in attic rooms,
      I was embarrassed, and he knew
to look away. We live in what is called *the habitable
   zone*. Pitching our orbit a little
to the north or south, we'd freeze, or burn.
   I know a man who'll tell you with conviction
      he's spoken with the aliens.
He weeps, "They challenge you. It isn't fun."
   Another man sits all day by the bank.
He speaks to anyone in riddles. "There's only one
   winner." "Who's that?" asks a stranger.
      "Think about it," he spits as a tag.
So the days go, the dead father resurrected, inert
   to animate, *hokus pokus*, the living

father put away, while radio telescopes
from west coast mountains beam hellos
to the heavens' solid or cloud-brightening
bodies. "Searched five close galaxies,
found nothing." "Searched all the sky,
found nothing." "Searched, found nothing."
The residents of the retirement home
join hands. Say they dance, tonight,
in a world they'd swear's not of their making,
born again, of God, or godless, dance
to kill the time. The prayers go up like static,
whole bloodlines, in thirty-zeroed combinations,
toward Epsilon Eridani, Alpha Centauri,
Orion, Zion, "Salem on the horizon . . ."
just as the dancers change the record.
Now they're moving in rhythm to the center
of the circle, their arms raised in
a bower through which one and then
another and then another passes,
passes, a little shyly, like a bride.


FOR CHARLIE

# *To the Angels*

We sit like the sparrows along the orchard's wall, the best
     of summer's stubble and stick-tights tangled
   in our hair. Due west the sun goes down,
    blinds us enough that the workers, emptying their sacks
     full of apples toward the harvest, are lifted
homeward across the dusty August heat-haze, like figures walking
     the shallow waters out to sea.
       It's a scene worth remembering,

now there are no longer angels, only the chaff
     from the milkweed that bears through the air the seeds,
   that lines the nests of warblers, and then is
  taken back, like down, losing, least of all, its name
     each autumn. But good-bye to the angels.
It was like us to create a thing more lonely than ourselves,
     as instinct poor, with wings.
       We used you up before we knew to give you

the retinal red and yellow fields belonging to the eyes
     of song birds that can navigate the world,
   those relentless, blackberry centers
  that pull the flocks, mindless of us, over the evening,
     like the negatives of stars.
But when you flew on your first day, maybe out of a cave
     painting, or out of a man turning flint to fire
     as a legion of gulls ascended,

you had no vector but the dust swept up in the thermals, rising,
     or the ragged clouds of monarchs
   riffling the sun, drifting, suicidal, over the ocean.
  Now in the airports and shopping malls emptied of any
     grace, their ceilings high as cathedrals,
their weather the dead buzzing of fluorescent nights and days,
     I think of you, think of your broken Botticellian hearts
     like the fake roses

my mother used to plant across the snow-crusted lawn
those years when spring was late, the trees slow
to blossom. Was it good that we could not make you
whole or real enough, who have survived in the shadows
the light makes coming through the leaves,
even as finally lost one day or exiled, you
climbed the air, flying on faith, sunblind
against the future,

but never so far from your beginnings that it was in your nature
to abandon us, or break, without home-
sickness above the clouds?

# Tartarchos

He dragged his ridgy, century-old carapace out of the mudhole
at Max Allen's Reptile Gardens one of our prison farm
apple picker's families ran, poachers mostly,
who'd already killed their only claim to fame,
a two-headed rattler, by trying to breed it with a cobra.
You could ride the tortoise for a dollar,
his dome grave-sized, almost.
An elephant driver's straddle, a lion tamer's whip

from the dusty giftshop, and we hobble-de-horsed the radius
of the chain that cuffed his leg, say ten feet over the piles
of rotting vegetables, the basalt bottomland along the Osage.
One spring evening, some years later, my sister
was beaten with a brush.
I ran from the house down to the pond, its clay-
baked hillside's erosion ruts deep enough to hide in.
Eye-level with the earth among the winter litter,

burr-twisted scarves no doubt the dogs had carried off, ditched
sleds, their runners rusting in the cattails,
I pulled something we called a flying saucer over me,
its shallow, muddied dish a little roof, and fell asleep.
It must have been about the time of sputnik,
citizens building bomb shelters,
claiming with characteristic fifties bitterness
their children would vacation on the moon.

In the tale of the Tontlawald an oyster shell, like Queequeg's
coffin, becomes a boat for the child the sea grows
up around, and sailors sing to her in passing.
Darwin and Melville, within ten years of each other on the Galapagos,
herded the tortoises into the nets, used them for ballast,
food for the long trip home, and filled their shells
with earth, like planets halved, raised birds-of-paradise mid-ocean.
O god of the underworld, o combs, brushes,

29

o ornamental dark in a king's crown, o lost Missouri tortoise. . . .
If you walk inland three days on one of the islands
following the paths the Spaniards first believed were roads
to the eternal city, you'll finally crest the hill above
their mating place, huge sky-colored pools
in which they bask by the hundreds, like stones you cannot help
but want to step across, or, with the sea behind you, balance
in the middle of, yourself the very compass, the point of view.

# Secrets

The lights in front of the hospital shine
as though the dark still harbored
secrets, as though there were a star,

invisible, called Heaven,
refracted in the brightly painted planets we hung,
as children, in our garage

or in the mirrored globes of the double helix
we built with ornaments and wire
and soda straws.

I love to imagine it now
half-fallen among my father's rusting tools,
my mother's wintering geraniums,

like Jacob's ladder, a tower
of Babel, its sprung connections breath
across a bottle when the wind blows

in under the doors.
Some nights, a thousand miles inland, a storm
blowing across the frozen fields,

I'd fall asleep pretending I heard the ocean,
heard the earth's ancient machinery's
creak and roar, the first myths gathering in the air

above the water like flocks pulled star
to star, prophesying,
in their spirals, hands gesturing toward language,

the neurons sparking as the animal
face contorts,
as the eyes burn into the eyes of the listener

and the lips spit, struggle
to form an O.
Now the early life's simple anthem turns

relentless, pleading, trapped
in the high octaves.
Now the egg quickens, sealing itself off, insisting

on its own more difficult
genetic music.
For the child born tonight under the comet's

ice and fire, born
near the century's end as though near the edge
of a continent, it's the dark

of a foreign year.
The air's full of fallout, the air that, transfigured,
becomes the voices of the millions

dead in the minds of the survivors.
It's the song you almost recognize, dreaming
in traffic of the afterlife,

dreaming the merciful past,
the lights by now
so many you hardly see the stars.

# Hall of Souls

Then everything came out of the drawers, down from the closets,
the nests from the chimney, the dust-mice whisked
from the corners. And from the several trunks, letters,
many undated, and the drafts of letters came,
and from the sills the empty bezels that were moths, a summer's
flies onto the naked wood, the rugs rolled up

and leaning like hillside trees against the windows up
three stories, eye-level with the maples that closeted
our rooms. Winters the boughs were lost ships rocking, summers,
billion-leaved. The sparrows in a mating frenzy whisked
themselves against the glass. Once one came
into Charlie's room and, lighting on a wet palette, lettered

the sill on his way out in reds and greens, lettered
the phone wire where, swaying from foot to foot, he seemed, up
high, to figure how suddenly that bluest ceiling had come
down on him, as if the hall of souls were really closet-
sized, and each descent, to which he sang, caught in a whisk
of sun or starlight, must be small enough to slip into a summer

window. Maybe that's why each year especially in summer
I've longed for our having a child. My letters
recount the terrible grip of someone's baby whisked
away too roughly in the supermarket and my own fear of closets.
I've lost it now, lost my mother's impulse to go up,
offering some toy, to that tired family, or if the child would come

to her, holding her, stroking her hair, until they'd come
to the register. I don't remember what happened after that. Summers
we slipped across the asphalt burning our feet. It's like stepping up
alone now onto an empty dance floor among the voices of our letters,
present tense, our old shoes, coats heaped from the closet.
It's like the day one late February when the wind whisked

the snow across the frozen pond where we walked, whisking
each other away from the dark spots each time the sun came
out, the light refracted under us, as if the ice held closets,
rooms, and we, who'll never own a house, strolled its summer
balconies imagining how we might furnish them—a desk for letter-
writing, a chair, a bed for sleeping in the open up-

stairs each summer of the afterlife—without clothes or closets,
our own letters put away, and you, come home at last, for good,
a little tired, whisking me up in your arms like you used to.

# To Science

The way love itself unravels like a toy-
sized double helix spiral
you could lay flat against the page
and take a ruler and draw in the staff
and score the DNA, surely
the genes have seasons.
The brown flecks in my mother's eyes
became my own, my son's, through adolescence.
The body knows, at most, an octave
of desire that meets the air sometimes
for nothing. Just thinking of your hands
I can go wet, or dreaming, come
in my sleep, and wake to a day
in which all men are liars, wearing clothes.

# *Media Years*

Then the tv evangelist out of West Covina
came on at six a.m., not before
        he'd wound up his fifteen or so monkeys,
    each with its own little cymbal
or drum, most of the mechanisms sprung, pitching
       the toys over as the camera
    faded in, as though the moral
        of that parable were entropy.—

               Maybe we'd been up all night
listening to the Muzak station, each deadly
    familiar song wrapped, it seemed, in cotton,
       between bulletins of the smog alerts,
   or the pile-ups, or the baby-lifts
       enroute from Saigon to L.A. Eclipsed in mountain
fires above the airstrips,
the sun rose like the end of the world,

       and all the animals
    were driven down into the valley. The residents
set traps—balanced orange crates
       at one end on sticks and put a little food inside.
All this for a photograph of something wild.
       Our neighbors caught the stunned red
         stare of a coyote
fleeing their garage. There's one of me

    in rollers stalking peacocks too tired or terrified
       to fly who grew so desperate
when I approached, stupidly offering water, seeds,
      we thought they'd break a wing
against Base housing's pink stucco walls.
As for the woman who took the picture,
      she was my friend.
    She'd drive in from the desert, stay

through the weekend, keep me
        company while my first husband flew
   what they called the system, outbound
          somewhere over the Pacific.
                  Near dawn on Sundays,
not wanting to go, or maybe more than ready,
    she'd fall into an imitation
         of her drunken father, spitting,

   waving her arms, her face changed so entirely,
         I had to look away.
Once my grounded-pilot-pentecostal neighbors lured me
in their back door for the laying on
         of hands. The prayer was, baptized
     in holy fire, I'd get the gift of tongues, rocking
to Johnny Cash among the tupperware
        and mushroom canisters, when in walked Trina

   with drugstore sherry and chocolate eclairs.
       Who can say why just now
          I'm remembering her
big childish body while I watch the residents
   of the retirement home next door walk out into
        the season's first snow?
They wander startled, otherworldly, clinging
      to one another's arms. It's nearly midnight.

She's dead a decade, driven, combing her hair,
across a median outside Palm Springs, the radio—
          beyond the crash, beyond her breathing—blaring
    some doped-up seventies chorus thousands
of voices on a freeway ten lanes wide just kept singing,
      like the oversoul, along to,
   on-ramp by on-ramp. In California
        there were mudslides, earthquakes.

There was a wind
named after a saint that swept the smog, each autumn,
   from the city of angels,
      and a woman who could recite in sequence
every exit from Tijuana to Riverside.
   Call her my blossoming.
Call them our media years. We wore bright dresses
with the backs cut out the time we read

     for nothing in a high school gym
   the first poems we'd written, where the bees swarmed
the hummingbird feeders in the eucalyptus
   and the air smelled of jet fuel and oranges
and the Air Force planes landed
     or took off, and someone in the groves
      turned the wicks down in the smudgepots,
after which, for luck, we burned the poems.

# Idaho Plates

Not to bless him, she lays her hands
on my son's head. *Yes,* she says
and *yes, he'll know some higher turn
in the spiral.* Stephen is surprised
to quieting. We're waiting
for our clothes to dry. Except for us,
the laundromat is empty. Outside the psychic's airstream trailer
flashes in the sun some signal
counterpoint to the small change,
zippers, buttons on all his shirts
and jackets hauled up by the lapels,
thrown down by the bully air, again
and again inside each cylinder.

# The Sea with Doors

Not the perfect preservation
of the body in ice nor the head bathed first
in tepid snow-water, but his face
as it wakes to an expression
of pain, as though his last delirium
could break again above the staff, a white
fire, into the highest octaves.
And when he's lifted, recognizable,
out of the frozen earth,
a young man, less than a hundred pounds,
yet in the flesh, a century
older, who is the seal-gloved
technician holding him against her
for the camera under the midnight sun?
And these mottled excavations, could
they be sudden multicolored islands
of happiness, an ancient autumn's air,
a smear of crystals caught in the pond-
dark shale? Is this the border
of eternity? some wronged season's visitation?
By the endless light his body's opened.
Weighed, one by one, his organs bleed the thaw.
But why is his face now turned away
from his own flowering in the domed tent,
his boy's genitals covered with a napkin,
who looks so nearly alive?
Is there no twilight, nothing
to stop the day here? As for the woman
laying out his clothes under the lamps in
the shape of him, shoeless, why does she finger
and finger each whale-bone button?
What time is it? What news beyond the years
that are less than the distance
his crew strayed off course? What now? Who

shut up the sea with doors
a thousand miles from the Northwest
Passage, that looks from here,
over the ice floes, like open sea?

# *House*

An Ohio blue-tip kitchen matchbox
             might have served as cradle in the one-room
attic-ceilinged house made, plane on plane,
of cloudy masonite, the only other furniture
             maybe a wood-block for a table,
         a Christmas ornament or two, a mirror shard.
But it was odd-sized, the miniature
             utterly lost in it, things scattered
through a field, while our old dolls would have been monstrous,
a flowering of limbs, their frayed lace half-slips
             too long, even for curtains for the one real
         fingerprinted pane,
         its sash nailed down to hold the wall together.
             The original inhabitants still ghosted the interior,
probably clothespin babies,
cardboard parents in crayola-button clothes,
             their faces vague, the way children have trouble
         drawing youth, or simply eyes.
It was a house that wanted nothing
             but to be viewed from the outside.
In the one art class in junior high
the first warm days in April, we'd taped butcher's paper
             to masonite squares, dipped brushes
         in the river, painted the prison
         along the south bluffs, silos like lighthouses
             across the ice floes, or the train depot
above which lived the county's only prostitute
and her deaf daughter. We'd seen the wigless,
             freshly painted heads hung up to dry
         on a masonite wall
         in the doll hospital, among the doctor's dented,
             grease-fuzzed pots and pans,
our dolls' lids closing, when we lay them on the counter,
over eyes of weighted socket-wire and glass,
             the whole contraption soldered,
         bridged like spectacles behind our Meg or Amy's

shattered forehead, magnified irises
like bluejay feathers.
Driving through Iowa one winter,
I glimpsed a woman running, coatless, from a barn toward a field
from which the late-feeding starlings rose
and broke above the highway
just as it began to snow, and I slowed
enough to see through the open stable door
a rafter-crossed high window, a reductive sky,
like the light that day in Bethany,
where two of my five grown sisters and I
circled the house
in a garage that overlooked the sea.
I held some faded satin flowers, two bunches
for a dollar, Eva, a Blue Willow
cup and saucer, but in the end, we put them down.

# Faith-Falling

Yes! My son has learned to fall by increments each day
backwards from the vaulting horse set just his height—his
    full weight—

into the bridge of arms extended by his classmates.
This means he'll trust the rope now that pins him to any
    mountain,

trust the least foothold, ice-slick, crumbling.
I like to imagine the times I've heard such cheers go up
    in school gymnasiums,

or stood, myself, at the cliff's edge, sounding, sounding.
I have a friend who taught me this week the work-a-day

of his disease, how not to sentimentalize his happiness—
in the morning radiation treatments, then lunch in the foot-
    hills,

where we spoke of the poem just out of reach, the one failed
    mostly, the one believed.
It's falling we do best, it's how we navigate the silence.

In the airplane on my way to him another passenger took
    snapshots,
turned on her knees in her seat behind First Class, aimed her
    camera at us all

and flashed and flashed. We smiled for her against the "chop,"
against the coffin-shaped fuselage, a hundred people, airsick,
    islanded, cresting

the thermals' high wakes, most of our dinner trays sent back
    untouched,
as from the dimmed rooms of a hospital. What could she hope for?

Surely the lighting's wrong, the angle foreshortening our faces,
already fear-blurred, bloated in the altitude.

Now somewhere in a darkroom, pinned frame by frame to the line,
we must look to be leaping out of ourselves,

like the Great Wallendas, who would have walked their doomed
high-wire formations over Europe, if they could.

It must have looked so easy drawn out across the sand,
that stick-figure genealogy, that human pyramid suspended in
        the long shadows

of winter quarters, the sawdust smell domestic between trailers,
the big cats dozing in their cages, the apes grooming their
        young.

Then even the children were given bars to practice
on the low wires toward the moment they'd balance on their
        parents' shoulders,

balanced, without a net, above the crowd.
When we touched down that night in California, we all applauded,

squeezed one another's hands. Terror had made us real enough
        to touch,
almost intimate, as we stepped from the jetway

flushed as performers from the wings, and he was waiting,
and he held me. On earth you can say good-bye.

# Kingdom, Phylum, Class, Order, Family, Genus, Species

Less than half the size
        of the Bernini angel, halfway
across the bridge, men, fleshy,
        scarred, animal-in-context, swear in three
           languages. Harnessed
    to the catafalco,
they can lean out only so far

  over the Tiber to draw
        up water in their buckets for
the work at hand, their safety
        ropes and pulleys, taut as fish-
           line or kitestring in the glare, caged
        as they are between the river
    and the sky. So light

  in years, they sand the wings.
        A white dust shadows their bodies,
ghosts tourists, pedestrians,
        as though, late in the millennium,
           some mortal ceiling
        had just been torn a-
way and we can't help but rise

  now and rise instead
        of fall in the full
sunlight still clinging to the scaffolding.

Deborah Digges was born in 1950 and raised in Jefferson City, Missouri. Her first book, *Vesper Sparrows,* was published in 1986 and won the Delmore Schwartz Memorial Award. She has been a fellow of the Ingram Merrill Foundation, the National Endowment for the Arts, and, most recently, the John Simon Guggenheim Foundation. She has two sons, Charles and Stephen, and lives in Massachusetts where she teaches at Tufts University.

## A NOTE ON THE TYPE

*This book is set in Linotype* ELECTRA, *a face designed by* W. A. DWIGGINS (1880–1956), *who was responsible for so much that is good in contemporary book design. Although much of his early work was in advertising and he was the author of the standard volume* Layout in Advertising, *Mr. Dwiggins later devoted his prolific talents to book typography and type design, and worked with great distinction in both fields. In addition to his designs for Electra, he created the Metro, Caledonia, and Eldorado series of type faces, as well as a number of experimental cuttings that were never issued commercially.*

*Electra cannot be classified as either modern or old-style. It is not based on any historical model, nor does it echo a particular period or style. It avoids the extreme contrast between thick and thin elements which marks most modern faces, and attempts to give a feeling of fluidity, power, and speed.*

Composed, printed, and bound by
Heritage Printers, Inc., Charlotte, North Carolina
Designed by Harry Ford